CHRISTMAS

The New Tes
in Pictures for Little Eyes

To *HEATHER WARKENTIN*

From S.S. TEACHERS
KATHY & SHAUNNA
HILDEBRANDT

The New Testament
in Pictures
for Little Eyes

by
Kenneth N. Taylor

MOODY PRESS · CHICAGO

© 1956, 1985, 1989 by Kenneth N. Taylor

The stories included in this book
have been extracted from
The Bible in Pictures for Little Eyes,
by Kenneth N. Taylor

1 2 3 4 5 6 Printing/ /Year 94 93 92 91 90 89

OTHER BOOKS BY KENNETH N. TAYLOR

Devotions for the Children's Hour
Stories for the Children's Hour
The Living Bible (Tyndale House Publishers)

Printed in England by Purnell Book Production Limited
Worldwide Co-edition organised and produced by Angus Hudson Ltd., London

Introduction

VEN LITTLE CHILDREN can understand great truths when told to them in simple words. And when pictures are added, doubly indelible impressions are made that can last forever.

No other book has changed so many lives so remarkably as the Bible. God's Word can be a source of light to childhood's earliest pathways if carefully presented. It can be a Rock to build a life on, even when that life is very small. "Give us a child until he is five years old," some say, "and his character will be formed forever."

It is incredibly important to begin *direct* Bible training at the earliest possible age, in addition to the influences surrounding the child from earliest days in a Christ-honoring home. This book can be read to children of approximate ages 3½ to 6 with great profit. Children of that age can understand with simple trust the great doctrines of God and His dealings with mankind. With simple trust they can accept and always believe what hardened, older minds find difficult.

It is the hope of author and publisher that this book will be a means of establishing little minds in truths from which nothing that will ever happen in the years ahead can shake them, because their trust will be in the Living God and in His Son, Jesus Christ our Lord.

CONTENTS

The New Testament
in Pictures for Little Eyes

 T IS NIGHTTIME and these men are out in the fields taking care of their sheep. They chase the bears away so that they will not eat the sheep. Can you see their sheep? But now what is happening? Who are these angels who have come? What are they saying? They are telling these men that God's Son has been born that night. He is a little baby. The angels are glad and the men are glad. They go quickly to the place where the baby is, so that they can pray to Him and thank God for Him.

QUESTIONS:

1. *Why are the men outside at night?*
2. *What are the angels telling them?*
3. *What do they decide to do?*

Luke 2:1-15

HE MEN WHO WERE TAKING CARE of the sheep have come to find God's Son. The angels told them where to find Him and now they have come to see the baby Jesus. There is the baby and His mother. The mother's name is Mary. God is the baby's Father. The men who are taking care of the sheep are worshiping the baby and thanking God that the baby is God's Son. The baby's name is Jesus.

QUESTIONS:

1. *Who is this baby?*
2. *Who is the baby's Father?*
3. *What is His mother's name?*

Luke 2:16-18

HO ARE THESE MEN? They are riding on camels. Have you ever seen a camel? Where are the men going in such a hurry? They are going to find God's Son. God has told them that His Son is going to be born. They are bringing many gifts to give Him. They know where to go because God has sent a star for them to follow. The star will take them to the baby Jesus.

QUESTIONS:

1. *Where are the men going?*
2. *How do they know where to go?*
3. *What is the name of God's Son?*

Matthew 2:1-9

16

HE MEN WHO WERE ON THE CAMELS have come a long way from another country. Now they have found the little baby they were looking for. They know that the baby is God's Son. They have brought many gifts to give Him. They are holding them out for Him to see while they worship Him and thank God. God is kind to these men to let them see His Son Jesus.

QUESTIONS:

1. *Are the men giving presents to the baby Jesus?*
2. *Can you see one of the camels?*

Matthew 2:10, 11

CAN YOU SEE THE OLD MAN in the picture who is holding the baby? He has waited all his life to see God's baby Son. The old man has asked Mary if he can hold Jesus. He has never been so happy in all his life before, because now at last Jesus is born and he can hold Him in his arms. He knows that Jesus will take care of God's people. The name of the lady standing behind him is Anna. God has told her, too, that this baby is His Son and she is very, very happy.

QUESTIONS:

1. *Why are the man and the lady so happy?*
2. *Is Jesus God's Son?*

Luke 2:25-38

 HIS IS ANOTHER PICTURE of Jesus. He has become a big boy now. In this picture we see the big men He is talking to. These old men are preachers and teachers. The boy Jesus is asking them questions and telling them things about God. These men cannot understand how a boy can know so much about God. They do not know that this boy is God's Son. This is Jesus.

QUESTIONS:

1. *Who is this boy?*
2. *Why are the men surprised?*
3. *Why does the boy know so much about God?*

Luke 2:40-52

HIS IS ANOTHER PICTURE of Jesus. Now He is a man. Another man whose name is John is pointing up to God and praying. John will baptize Jesus. Jesus is glad because God wants John to do this. As soon as Jesus is baptized He will hear a voice from the sky saying, "This is my Son and I love Him. Listen to what He tells you to do." Do you know where the voice will come from? It will be God talking to Jesus and the other people who are watching him. God wants everyone to know that this is His Son.

QUESTIONS:

1. *What is John doing to Jesus?*
2. *Where will the voice come from?*
3. *What will the voice say?*

Matthew 3:13-17

24

**ESUS HAS GONE FAR AWAY.** There are no other people here to help Him or to make Him happy. He is alone. He has not eaten anything for breakfast, or lunch, or supper. He did not eat anything yesterday or the day before that. He has not eaten anything for forty days. Soon Satan, God's enemy, will come and try to get Jesus to do something bad but Jesus will not listen to bad Satan. Jesus is God's Son and He is good. He has never done anything bad at all. He will never listen to Satan. Jesus listens only to God His Father and does only what God says.

QUESTIONS:

1. *Why is Jesus hungry?*
2. *Will He ever do anything bad?*
3. *Who will try to get Jesus to be bad?*

Matthew 4:1-11

502

ESUS ASKS TWELVE MEN to be His special friends. These men are called His disciples. They go with Jesus wherever He goes and help Him in all His work. These men are happy because Jesus has asked them to help Him. Some of the names of these men are Peter, John, James, Thomas, and Andrew. These twelve men are Jesus' helpers.

QUESTIONS:

1. *Who are these men?*
2. *Will they help Jesus?*
3. *Do you know any of their names?*

Mark 3:13-19

NE DAY JESUS was at a big dinner where a lady was getting married. After a while they needed more grape juice for the people to drink. They ask Jesus what to do. Jesus tells them to fill up six big jars of water and tells them to take them to the man. And do you know what? It wasn't water any more. It was better than they had ever tasted. Jesus can do things like that because He is God.

QUESTIONS:

1. *What did the people ask Jesus to do?*
2. *What did Jesus tell them to do with the big jars?*
3. *Can Jesus help us when we need Him?*

John 2:1-11

ESUS IS MAKING SOME MEN go out of the church. They didn't come to church to love God and pray. No, they are doing things there that God does not want them to do. They are selling things to get a lot of money and be rich. They don't love God and don't want to pray. Jesus has a whip in His hand and the men are afraid of Him. He tells them to take all of those things away. He says that they are in His Father's house and they must not do things like that when they are there.

QUESTIONS:

1. *What does Jesus have in His hand?*
2. *What does Jesus want these men to do?*

John 2:13-17

O YOU SEE JESUS standing there? He told Peter to throw his fishing net in the water. Peter did not think that there would be any fish but he did what Jesus told him to do, and now just see how many fish there are! Peter minded Jesus and now Peter has all these fish. Can you see all the fish? There are almost too many to count. Peter and his friends don't know what to do with all of them. They have so many in their boat that it is almost sinking. They give some to the men in the other boat and it is almost sinking too. Where did all these fish come from?

QUESTIONS:

1. *Who told Peter to catch the fish?*
2. *Can you count how many fish there are, or are there too many?*

Luke 5:1-11

WHAT IS HAPPENING HERE? Look at the men at the top of the picture. They brought their friend to Jesus. They have taken away part of the roof of the house and put him down right in front of Jesus where He will be sure to see him. The man could not walk and was lying on his bed. Can you see his bed? They brought him to Jesus because they want him to walk again. Jesus tells the man to get well and now he is standing up. He has already learned to walk. Jesus makes him well right away.

QUESTIONS:

1. *How did the men get their friend down to Jesus?*
2. *Could the man walk before?*
3. *What did Jesus do?*

Luke 5:17-26

36

T IS NIGHTTIME and Jesus is talking to a man whose name is Nicodemus. Can you say, "Nicodemus"? He is a good man but he does not know that Jesus is God's Son and he doesn't know very much about God. Jesus is telling him about God. He is telling him how to get to Heaven. He says, "Nicodemus, you cannot get there by yourself but God will take you there if you believe in Me. God loves you, Nicodemus." Jesus died so that Nicodemus could go to Heaven. Jesus died so that you and I can go to Heaven if we love Him.

QUESTIONS:

1. *What is this man's name?*
2. *Did he know God?*
3. *Why did Jesus have to die?*

John 3:1-5, 14-18

HIS MAN IS GLAD because his little boy feels all better again. Yesterday he was so sick that he didn't want to run and play. He only wanted to be there in his bed. His father was sad. He went to see Jesus. He asked Jesus to come and make the little boy well. Jesus said that He would help. He told the father to go home and the little boy would be all right. Jesus is far away but He makes the little boy well again.

QUESTIONS:

1. *Was the little boy sick?*
2. *Is he sick now?*
3. *Where is Jesus?*

John 4:46-54

40

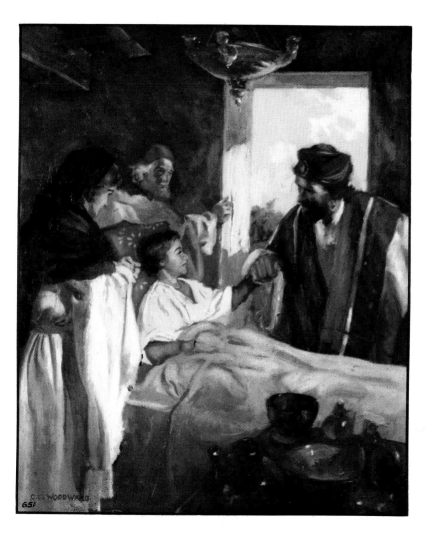

ESUS IS TALKING TO THE PEOPLE. See how many of them there are! They want to hear what Jesus says. They know Jesus is their Friend and they want to mind Him. He is telling the people to be kind and good. He tells them not to quarrel. Some of these people will love Jesus always and some of them will go away from Him and not want Him to be their Friend any more. Isn't that too bad? If Jesus is not their Friend, then God will not let them come to Heaven. Jesus wants to be your Friend too.

QUESTIONS:

1. *Who is talking to the people?*
2. *Is Jesus your Friend?*

Matthew 5:1-11

ESUS TOLD A STORY about two men who built houses. One of them built his house on the sand. He was a foolish man. It rained and rained and all of the sand washed away and the house fell down. The other man built his house upon a rock. Even though it rains the rock will not wash away. He is a wise man because he built his house upon a rock.

QUESTIONS:

1. *Was it a good idea to build a house on the sand?*
2. *What happened to that house?*
3. *When it rained did the house on the rock fall down?*

Matthew 7:24-29

ESUS IS HELPING A MAN SIT UP. The man was dead and his mother was sad. Jesus saw the mother crying. He went over to see the man lying on the bed. The man could not move. He was dead. Jesus tells him to be alive again. When Jesus says that, all of a sudden the man begins to move. He opens his eyes and sees Jesus and he sees his mother too. The man and his mother are glad and Jesus is glad too.

QUESTIONS:

1. *Was the man dead?*
2. *What did Jesus tell him to do?*
3. *Then what happened?*

Luke 7:11-16

ESUS AND HIS FRIENDS are in a boat. It is at night. There is a great storm. The wind is blowing. It is raining hard. The friends are afraid the ship will sink and they will all be drowned. Is Jesus afraid? No, He isn't. No, because He knows His God will take care of them. Jesus is standing up and holding up His hands and now the storm is going away. Jesus tells the storm to stop and it did.

QUESTIONS:

1. *Is Jesus afraid?*
2. *What is He doing?*
3. *What will happen to the storm?*

Matthew 8:23-27

HIS LITTLE GIRL is twelve years old. She was very sick and her father went to find Jesus. He asked Jesus to come and make his little girl well again. The doctors couldn't get her better, but he knows Jesus can. Jesus comes and takes the little girl's hand and says, "Get up, little girl." Right away she sits up and gets out of bed and starts to play and she is all right again. The little girl died but Jesus brought her back to life and gave her to her mother and father. That is why they are so surprised and happy.

QUESTIONS:

1. *Why are the mother and father so happy?*
2. *How did Jesus make the little girl well?*

Mark 5:22-43

50

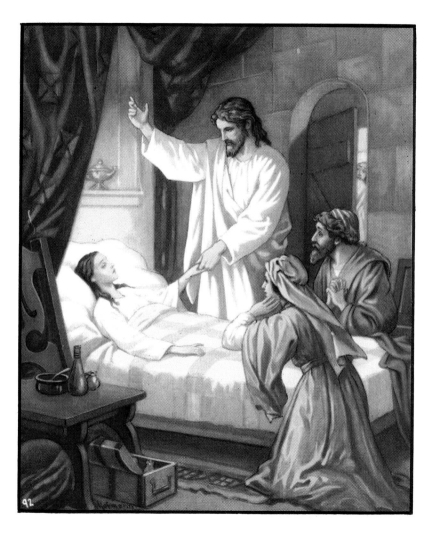

JESUS IS TALKING here with a man who cannot see Him. The man is blind. His eyes are hurt so that he cannot see anything at all. Close your eyes now and you can tell what it is like to be blind. Everything is dark. Someone told this man Jesus was coming. The man heard Jesus coming. Then he cried out very loudly, "Jesus, please help me. Please make my eyes well so that I can see." Jesus touches his eyes and says, "Be open." And right away his eyes are all right and he can see. Isn't Jesus a wonderful Friend?

QUESTIONS:

1. *Could the man see Jesus?*
2. *What did Jesus say to make his eyes open?*

Matthew 9:27-31

THIS POOR MAN lying on the ground was going on a trip, and all of a sudden some men came and took away his money and some of his clothes and hurt him and ran away. They left him lying there on the road. Some people he knew came walking by but they wouldn't stop to help him. They just looked at him and went on. Then a man he didn't like came along and stopped. You can see him in the picture helping the poor man who is hurt. He is pouring some medicine on some places and soon he will lift him up and put him on his donkey and take him to a hotel. Jesus wants us to be kind to everyone, even people who hit us or don't like us.

QUESTIONS:

1. Why is the man lying there?
2. What is the other man doing?

Luke 10:30-37

ARY IS SITTING DOWN listening while Jesus is talking to her. He is telling her many things that she needs to know. Do you see the other lady, the one who is standing up? Her name is Martha. She is Mary's sister. She is getting supper ready. Martha is working very hard and wants Mary to help her instead of talking to Jesus. Martha asks Jesus to make Mary help her get the supper. But Jesus says, "No, let Mary sit here and listen, because that is even more important than getting supper." Did you know that it is more important to listen to Jesus than it is to eat?

QUESTIONS:

1. Who are these two ladies?
2. What does the one standing up want the other one to do?
3. Did Jesus say that Mary should keep on listening to Him?

Luke 10:38-42

56

ESUS IS ANGRY with these men. He is talking to them while they are eating their dinners. He is angry because they say that they love God and they really don't. They say that they want to mind God, but they are telling lies because they want to do things their own way instead of the way God says. They give money to God but they do not love Him. They go to God's house but they do not love God. That is why Jesus is angry. He wants them to love God. He does not want their money unless they love Him.

QUESTIONS:

1. *Why is Jesus angry with these men?*
2. *Do these men love God?*
3. *Do they give money to God?*
4. *Does God want their money if they do not love Him?*

Luke 11:37-44

THIS MAN IS A RICH FARMER. He has lots of money. He is looking at his barns. Do you see his men putting hay into the barns? But this man does not love God. He loves his money and his farm more than he loves God. He has so much money and food that he doesn't know where to put it so he is going to build a bigger barn. But tonight God will let this rich man die so he will not wake up tomorrow morning. He can't use all his food in the barn any more because he will die tonight and never come back. God will take him away. The man is bad because he loves his farm but doesn't love God.

QUESTIONS:

1. *Does this man have lots of things?*
2. *Does this man love God?*

Luke 12:16-21

ESUS IS TALKING to His friends. Do you see the pretty flower He is pointing to? Jesus is telling them to look at the flowers. The flowers don't work hard to cook their suppers, do they? No, flowers don't need to cook and work hard, because God takes care of them. They don't need fine clothes, because God has made them grow with their beautiful clothes right on them. Jesus is telling His friends that God takes care of the flowers and He will take care of them too if they ask Him, and do whatever He says.

QUESTIONS:

1. *What is Jesus showing the disciples?*
2. *Will God take care of you?*

Luke 12:27-32

THIS MAN IS PLANTING SEEDS. He is carrying them in his bag over his shoulder. He throws the little seeds out on the ground. He wants them to grow and become soft green grass. He wants them to become big plants. Oh, look, do you see the birds behind him? They are eating up some of the seeds. Those seeds will not grow because the birds are taking them away. Some of the seed is falling down on the rocks and thorns. Can you see the thorns? The seeds cannot grow there very well. But some of the seeds fall on good ground and will grow up and become big plants.

QUESTIONS:

1. *Will the seed grow on the rock?*
2. *Where will the seed grow best?*

Matthew 13:3-8

OOK AT ALL THESE PEOPLE. See how many there are? They are all hungry. They have not had any lunch and now it is time for supper and they don't have anything to eat. One boy brought his lunch so he will not be hungry. He would be glad to give his lunch to all the people but do you think that would be enough for them to eat? No, of course not. The boy is giving his lunch to Jesus. Jesus will break the bread in pieces and give the pieces to His helpers, and do you know what will happen then? Jesus makes the bread grow so that there will be enough for everyone.

QUESTIONS:

1. *What is the boy doing with his lunch?*
2. *What will Jesus do with it?*

Matthew 14:15-23

HAT IS HAPPENING in this picture? There is water with a boat in it and there are some men in the boat. Do you see Jesus in the picture? Is He swimming in the water? No, He is walking on top of it. Can you walk on top of water in your bathtub? No, of course not. But Jesus made the water. He can stand on it if He wants to. One of the men in the boat is Peter. When Peter sees Jesus on the water he wants to walk on it too. Peter will step out on the water and start to walk toward Jesus. Then he will become frightened and begin to sink, and Jesus will come and save him.

QUESTIONS:

1. *Can Jesus walk on top of the water?*
2. *Will Peter walk part of the way on top of the water?*
3. *When Peter gets scared, then what will happen?*

Matthew 14:22-33

710

**J**ESUS IS TALKING to Peter and James and John. They are up on a high mountain. No one else is there. All of a sudden Jesus' clothes begin to shine and become brighter and brighter, and whiter than snow. Peter and James and John are frightened. Then all of a sudden they see two other men standing there talking to Jesus. You can see them there in the picture. These two men are Moses and Elijah who lived long ago. They have come down from Heaven to talk to Jesus. They are talking about how some bad men are going to take Jesus and hurt Him and kill Him. Soon Moses and Elijah will go away again and a bright cloud will come over above where Jesus is standing. God's voice will talk out of the cloud and say, "Jesus is My Son, listen to Him."

QUESTIONS:

1. *What color did Jesus' clothes become?*
2. *Who came to talk with Jesus?*
3. *What did the voice in the cloud say?*

Matthew 17:1-9

AZARUS IS JESUS' FRIEND. One day Lazarus got sick and died. Jesus wasn't there to make him well again. The friends of Lazarus took his body and put it in the hole in the big rock and covered the hole so that no one could go in or out. When Jesus came he told the men to roll away the stone, and Jesus prayed and asked God to make Lazarus alive. Now can you see what is happening in this picture? Lazarus is coming out again. He was dead but now he is alive. Do you know why? It is because Jesus is there.

QUESTIONS:

1. *Did Jesus make the man alive?*
2. *Are the people glad that Jesus came?*

John 11:1-45

CLEVELAND
WOODWARD

ESUS LOVES LITTLE CHILDREN. In this picture He is holding some of them on His lap and talking to them. Once Jesus' friends tried to send the children away. They thought that Jesus didn't want children around Him. Jesus talked to the disciples and told them never to say things like that. He wants the children to be with Him. He says, "Let the little children come to Me. Do not send them away because I love them and want them with Me."

QUESTIONS:

1. *What is Jesus holding in His arms?*
2. *Does Jesus love little children?*
3. *Are you a little child?*
4. *Does Jesus love you?*

Matthew 19:13-15

74

 ESUS IS CRYING. He is looking at the old city of Jerusalem. There are many people in this city where He is looking. They do not love Jesus or His Father. They do not know that Jesus is God's Son. Jesus knows that some day a great army will come and knock down their city. If these people would only believe in Jesus then these terrible things would not happen to them. Jesus loves them and wants to help them, but they do not love Jesus and that is why He is crying.

QUESTIONS:

1. *What is Jesus looking at?*
2. *Why is He crying?*

Luke 13:31-35

76

THE MAN IN THE PICTURE has lost one of his sheep. It ran away and fell down and couldn't get back up again. The little sheep is lost and crying and helpless. The man went to find him and finally he is there picking it up. He will take it home and get it all warm again and get it something to eat. The man in the picture is good because he takes care of the sheep. The man looks like Jesus. Jesus wants to take care of us when we get lost. Jesus loves you very much. You can be one of His little lambs.

QUESTIONS:

1. *How did the little sheep get there?*
2. *What is the man doing?*

Luke 15:3-7

78

THIS LADY IS PUTTING PERFUME on Jesus' feet and then wiping it off with her hair. The perfume has cost a lot of money. The men sitting at the table with Jesus are telling Him that the lady shouldn't do this but Jesus is glad. He wants her to use the perfume because she is doing it to tell Jesus, "Thank You." Jesus has been kind to her. She has done many bad things but Jesus will forgive her. Jesus will die for her sins. She is glad that He is so kind and so she has put the perfume on His feet to tell Him, "Thank You." Jesus died for you, too. Have you told Him, "Thank You"?

QUESTIONS:

1. *Where did the lady put the perfume?*
2. *Was Jesus glad?*
3. *Have you ever told Jesus, "Thank You," for what He has done for you?*
4. *Shall we thank Him now?*

John 12:1-7

THIS BOY IS GOING AWAY from home. He is saying good-by to his father. Now he will jump on his horse and ride away. His father is sorry because he doesn't want the boy to go away. But the boy thinks it will be more fun away from home. He asks his father to give him a lot of money and now he will go away. Are you sorry that the boy is so bad? He should have stayed at home and worked and helped his father instead of going away.

QUESTIONS:

1. *Did the boy want to stay home or go away?*
2. *Is the father happy or sad?*

Luke 15:11-19

I N THIS PICTURE you can see the man who went away from his house even when his father didn't want him to. Now he has come back home again. He is sitting in a big chair and his father is very happy. After he went away he began to get very hungry and so he decided to come home again. His father is glad to see him. He didn't know if his father would want him to come back, but you can see how happy the father is to see him again. When the father saw him he ran and welcomed him and is telling him how glad he is.

QUESTIONS:

1. *Did the father let the boy come home?*
2. *Is the boy happy?*
3. *Is the father happy?*

Luke 15:20-24

**D**O YOU SEE THESE MEN who are walking away from Jesus? They were lepers. That means that they were very sick. Everyone was afraid to go near them because they were so sick. People who touched them might get sick too. When they saw Jesus they called to Him and said, "Jesus, help us. Please help us." Jesus saw them and heard them calling. He wanted to help them and He made all of them well. He healed them all but only one of them came back to tell Him, "Thank You." This man is so glad he is well again that he falls down in front of Jesus. All the others forgot to tell Jesus, "Thank You."

QUESTIONS:

1. *Were all these men sick?*
2. *Who healed them?*
3. *What is the man in the picture doing?*
4. *Have you thanked Jesus because He is your Friend?*

Luke 17:11-19

HY IS THIS MAN LYING HERE so still? It is because he is dead. His father owns that house but some other people are living there. His father sent his son to get the rent money from the people staying in the house but the people wouldn't give the money to him. Instead they hurt him and killed him and threw him out on the ground where you can see him lying. What do you think the father will do when he hears about this? He will come and get the policeman, and they will catch the people who live in this house and take them off to jail, because of the terrible thing they have done to his son.

QUESTIONS:

1. *Who owns this house?*
2. *What did the man's father send him to get?*
3. *What did the people do?*

Matthew 21:33-41

88

**J**ESUS IS SITTING in God's house watching the people putting money into a box. They are giving this money to God. In the picture you can see a lady who doesn't have very much money. She has brought a few pennies. That is all the money she has, and she is giving it all to God. When she puts this in she will not have any more money left at all. She is giving God everything that she has. Jesus is glad because the lady loves God so much. He doesn't think the rich men standing there have given very much at all. They have put in lots and lots of money but they are still rich and have lots more money left for themselves at home. Jesus says the poor woman's few pennies are better than all the money from the rich people who don't love Him.

QUESTIONS:

1. *Did the rich men put in a lot of money?*
2. *How much does the poor lady have left after she puts in her money?*

Mark 12:41-44

**VERYONE IS HAPPY** because Jesus has come to visit them. He has come to the city of Jerusalem. All the people think he has come to Jerusalem to be their king. They want Jesus to be king because He is so kind to them and can help them. See how some people are putting their coats on the ground for Jesus to ride over. Others are cutting down branches from the trees and making a path for Him. The people shout and thank God because they think Jesus will help them all be rich and have lots of money and other things that they don't have now. They do not know that Jesus will soon be killed.

QUESTIONS:

1. *Are the people happy?*
2. *What are they putting down on the road for Jesus to ride over?*
3. *Why are they doing this?*

John 12:12-19

148

HERE IN THIS PICTURE you can see Jesus talking to some of His friends. He is telling them about what is going to happen to Him. He is pointing up to Heaven, telling them that soon He will go there to be with God His Father. Jesus says that some day all His friends will come to Heaven too and live there with Him always.

QUESTIONS:

1. Where is Jesus pointing?
2. What is He telling His friends?

Luke 22:14-22

94

HIS MAN HAS MADE a great dinner and is ready to eat it. Can you see the man pointing to the food on the table? But who is coming to eat it? The man asked many of his rich friends to come and have dinner with him but they wouldn't. They didn't know what a wonderful dinner it was going to be so they said they had other things to do and couldn't come. Then the man invited the poor people who were sick and crippled and blind. Do you see them coming? They are glad to come and eat. Soon the table will be full of people. The man is glad because of his new friends but he is sorry because of those who would not come. Jesus wants you to come and live with Him some day. Will you be glad to come?

QUESTIONS:

1. *Who did the man invite at first to come and eat the good dinner?*
2. *Did the people he asked first want to come?*
3. *Who finally came to the dinner?*
4. *Does Jesus want you to come to Him?*

Matthew 22:1-14

OME MEN ARE ASKING Jesus a question. They want to know what is the most important rule for them to mind. Can you think what that rule would be? Would it be to eat nicely? Or would it be not going across the street alone? No. These things are very important and you should eat nicely and must be careful about cars or you will get into trouble. But there is something even more important that we should do. Jesus tells these men what it is. He says that the greatest thing for them to do is to always love God. Do you love God? Do you do whatever He says? What are some things God wants you to do?

QUESTIONS:

1. *What is the most important rule to mind?*
2. *What are some things God wants you to do?*
3. *Do you love God by doing what He says?*

Matthew 22:35-40

**W**HAT IS HAPPENING IN this picture? Jesus has a loaf of bread in His hand. He is breaking it into pieces. He will give these pieces to His disciples who are sitting there at the supper table. Jesus will tell them to eat the bread. He says that the bread is His body. Jesus is telling His disciples that He must soon die. He died for you. He died for me. We have done bad things that God must punish. But Jesus asked to be punished for you. God punished Jesus instead of you. Jesus didn't do anything bad but God punished Him. Do you know why?

QUESTIONS:

1. *What does Jesus have in His hand?*
2. *Who will eat the bread?*
3. *What is going to happen to Jesus?*

Luke 22:14-20

ESUS IS TALKING to His disciples. He is telling them what is going to happen to Him. Some men are going to take Him and kill Him but Jesus tells them not to be afraid. He says that God will take care of them. Jesus tells them that He will go away to His Father, away up in Heaven. When He gets there He will get places ready for them to come to live. He is getting a place ready for you to live in Heaven too, if you love Jesus.

QUESTIONS:

1. *What is Jesus telling them?*
2. *Where is Jesus now?*

John 14:1-14

J ESUS IS PRAYING all alone. He is in a garden and it is night. He is talking to His Father in Heaven. Jesus is very,very sad because He knows what will happen to Him soon. He knows that some men will come to get Him and take Him away and nail Him to a cross so that He will die. He will die on the cross so that God will not need to punish you and me for the bad things we have done. Jesus is sad because He does not want to die. He doesn't need to, either. He could ask God to send the angels to take care of Him but He will let the men kill Him. Jesus is glad to die for you.

QUESTIONS:

1. *Is Jesus happy or sad?*
2. *What is going to happen to Him?*

Luke 22:39-48

**D**ID YOU EVER HEAR about a man named Judas Iscariot? Judas pretended that he was one of Jesus' friends. Some bad men said they would give Judas lots of money if he would help them catch Jesus. In this picture Judas is bringing them to where Jesus is. It is night. They are bringing torches. Do you see the torches in their hands, giving light? They don't have flashlights and so they use these torches instead. Is Jesus going to run away from them? No, Jesus is standing, waiting. He could go away if He wanted to, but He will let them take Him.

QUESTIONS:

1. *What is the name of the man leading these bad people to Jesus?*
2. *Why doesn't Jesus run away?*

Luke 22:47-54

106

**ETER IS ONE** of Jesus' friends and disciples. He is getting warm by being near the fire with some other people. Peter looks angry. The lady is pointing at him but he is telling this lady, "No." Why is he saying that? This lady has asked Peter if Jesus is his Friend. Peter tells her, "No." He says that he doesn't know Jesus at all. What a bad thing to say. Peter is telling a lie because he is afraid the other people there will hurt him if they know he is Jesus' friend. Soon he will look up and see Jesus looking at him and then he will cry because he has done such a bad thing.

QUESTIONS:

1. Was Peter a friend of Jesus?
2. What did Peter tell the girl?

John 18:10-27

OW THE PEOPLE HAVE TAKEN JESUS to a man whose name was Pilate. Pilate can let them kill Jesus or else make them let Jesus go. He is talking to the people and telling them that he thinks he ought to let Jesus go. He says Jesus is good. He tells them that Jesus hasn't done anything bad at all. See how angry the people are! They want Pilate to let them kill Jesus. They are shouting at Pilate and Pilate is afraid of them. Soon he will decide to give Jesus to the men so that they can kill Him.

QUESTIONS:

1. *What is this man's name?*
2. *What do the people want Pilate to do?*
3. *What will Pilate do?*

John 19:1-16

THE BAD MEN have taken Jesus up the hill and have nailed His hands and His feet on these big pieces of wood so that He will die after a while. Can you think what it would be like if you were hanging there with nails through your hands? Oh, what a terrible thing they are doing to Jesus! Do you know why Jesus was nailed there? It is because He loves you and me. You and I have done bad things and God should punish us. But God doesn't want to do that because He loves us. God sent His dear Son Jesus who wanted to be punished for us. In this picture you can see Jesus being punished for your sins by dying there on the cross. That is how much Jesus loves you. He died for you.

QUESTIONS:

1. *What are in Jesus' hands?*
2. *Why did Jesus let them kill Him?*
3. *Does Jesus love you?*

John 19:16-24

112

ESUS IS DEAD. His body is all wrapped up in a white cloth. His friends are putting His body into a great hole in the rock. Soon they will leave Him there all alone. They do not think they will ever see Jesus again. They will go away and leave Him here because He is dead. How sad they are! They do not know that soon He will become alive again and come out of the place where they are putting Him. Jesus is dead but God is going to bring Him back to life.

QUESTIONS:

1. *Where are they putting Jesus' body?*
2. *Will His body stay there in the hole?*

John 19:40-42

114

THESE THREE LADIES are Jesus' friends. They have come to His grave to put some sweet perfume on the clothes He was wrapped up in after He died. They thought this would be a nice thing to do even though Jesus was dead and couldn't smell the perfume. Then they would sadly go away and leave Jesus there and never see Him again. But what is happening? An angel is inside the grave where Jesus was. The angel tells them Jesus isn't there! Jesus is alive and has gone away! Jesus was dead, but God made Him alive again! Jesus said this would happen, but no one believed Him. Now His friends know that whatever Jesus says is always true. He says that He will make all His friends alive again after they are dead. He will take them up to Heaven to be with Him always and always. Are you one of Jesus' friends? Aren't you glad that Jesus is alive?

QUESTIONS:

1. Who are these three ladies?
2. Who is talking to them?
3. What is he telling them?

Mark 16:1-8

116

AT LAST some of Jesus' friends are meeting Him again. They are very surprised. They thought Jesus was dead. They didn't know that Jesus was alive again. They are walking along and they see somebody standing there, and it is Jesus! How surprised and happy they are. They know now that Jesus is God's Son and they fall down at His feet and pray to Him. Jesus is saying, "Don't be afraid. Go and tell My other friends to go to a certain place and I will meet them there."

QUESTIONS:

1. *Who are these ladies talking to?*
2. *Why are they surprised and happy?*

John 20:11-18

DO YOU SEE THESE TWO MEN running as fast as they can? One of them is Peter and the other one is John. Peter is the older man and John is younger. Why are they running so fast? It is because the women have told them that Jesus is not in the grave but is alive again. Peter and John can hardly believe what the women have told them and they are going to see for themselves. They do not understand how Jesus could be alive and not in the hole in the rock. What an exciting morning this was when Jesus came back to life again!

QUESTIONS:

1. *Who are these two men?*
2. *Where are they going?*
3. *What will they find out?*

John 20:1-5

PETER AND JOHN ran right into the place where Jesus had been buried. In the picture you can see Peter inside, looking for Jesus. Is Jesus there? No, the cloth that was wrapped around Jesus is lying there, but Jesus has come out and gone away. He is alive again and isn't in the grave. Peter is surprised. John is surprised too. John is standing outside looking in. Finally they know that Jesus is not dead any more.

QUESTIONS:

> 1. *Which man is Peter?*
> 2. *Where is Jesus?*

John 20:6-10

HREE MEN ARE WALKING along a road. Two of them are going to their home. When the third man came along and asked them why they were so sad they said it was because Jesus was dead. The third man began to tell them more about Jesus and why He had to die. He told them that Jesus died for their sins. The two men are asking this third man to come and eat with them. While they were eating, all of a sudden they realized that the third man was Jesus. They had been talking to Jesus and didn't know it! As soon as they knew this, suddenly Jesus disappeared and wasn't eating there with them any more. He had gone away.

QUESTION:

1. Who is the third man?

Luke 24:13-32

THE DISCIPLES WERE TALKING together when all of a sudden Jesus was standing there with them. He hadn't knocked or come in at the door. He was just there! He must have come right through the walls because Jesus can do anything. His disciples were scared but Jesus says, "Don't be afraid, I am Jesus." In this picture you can see Him showing His friends the holes in His hands and His feet, so that they will know that this is really their very own Jesus who was nailed to the big pieces of wood and died. Now He is alive again and they are seeing Him. Pretty soon He will eat some fish with them and some honey, so that they will know that He is really alive and is not just a ghost.

QUESTIONS:

1. *Who is the man talking to the disciples?*
2. *Did He open the door and come in?*

Luke 24:33-48

126

NE DAY WHILE JESUS was talking with His disciples out on a hill, all of a sudden He began to go up into the air. Do you see the cloud there above Him? Jesus goes into the cloud and they will not see Him any more. Do you know where He is going? He is going to Heaven to live again with God His Father. When Jesus has gone away, two angels will come and talk with Jesus' friends and tell them that Jesus will come back again some day. Some day Jesus is going to come and take all His friends to Heaven. Are you one of Jesus' friends?

QUESTIONS:

1. *Where is Jesus going?*
2. *Will He come back again?*

Acts 1:9-11

 NE DAY WHILE JESUS' FRIENDS were praying together, there came a noise that sounded like a big wind coming from the sky, and the noise was all around them in the house, although they couldn't feel any wind. Do you see what is on the men's heads? It looks like tongues made of fire on each of them. Why is this happening? It is because God the Holy Spirit is coming down upon these men. After a while the tongues of fire will go away but the Holy Spirit will stay in their hearts. The Holy Spirit will help them and tell them many things and make them very strong. Jesus sent the Holy Spirit to comfort and help them.

QUESTIONS:

1. What is on the men's heads?
2. Who is coming into these men?
3. Who sent the Holy Spirit to them?

Acts 2:1-3

130

**P**ETER IS TALKING to all of these other people who don't know about Jesus yet. He is telling them that Jesus wants to be their friend and their Saviour. They have come from all over the world. Peter is telling them about how Jesus died and came back to life. These people come from a different country, but Peter is talking to them in their own language. God is helping Peter and the other disciples to talk in whatever language they need to tell people about Jesus. When these people hear about Jesus dying for them they are sad and ask what they should do. Peter told them to believe on the Lord Jesus, and many of them did.

QUESTIONS:

1. *What is Peter telling these people?*
2. *Do they decide to love Jesus?*

Acts 2:4-8, 14-21

PETER AND JOHN have come to God's house to pray. A man is sitting there who can't walk. Something is the matter with his legs. He was that way when he was a tiny baby and he has never been able to walk. That is why he is sitting there near God's house asking people to give him money to buy food. When he sees Peter and John he asks them to give him some money. Peter says he didn't have any, but he could give him something else that was a lot better. He says, "Get up and walk. Jesus will make you well." In the picture you can see the man beginning to get up. He will walk and run. He will give thanks to God.

QUESTIONS:

1. *Could this man walk before Peter talked to him?*
2. *Where is Jesus?*
3. *Did Jesus help Peter make the man walk?*

Acts 3:1-11

134

**P**ETER IS TALKING to the bad men who killed Jesus. They don't like Peter and would like to kill him. They are angry because Peter made the man walk, who was sitting on the steps of the church. In the picture you can see the man standing there with Peter. Peter tells them that Jesus made the man well again. They are telling Peter not to talk about Jesus any more and Peter isn't minding them. Peter minds God, but not these men, so he will keep on telling how kind and wonderful Jesus is.

QUESTIONS:

    1. Do the bad people want Peter to talk about Jesus?

    2. Will Peter stop talking about Jesus?

Acts 4:5-21

HE MAN LYING DOWN on the floor is dead. The man standing up is Peter. Peter was sitting there and the man came in and told him a lie. As soon as he told the lie he suddenly fell down and died. God punished Ananias because he told a lie. Soon the people will carry him outside and make a hole and put him in it and cover him up.

QUESTIONS:

1. *Why is the man there on the floor?*
2. *Did he tell a lie to God?*

Acts 5:1-11

**P**ETER IS IN JAIL. The bad people who killed Jesus have put him there. The doors and windows are all locked so that he can't get out. He has been there all night. Here in this picture you can see Peter lying there in jail when all of a sudden an angel comes. The angel is waking Peter up and telling him to come with him. The angel will unlock the doors of the jail. The angel doesn't have a key but he will open the doors anyway. When he is safely out he will tell Peter to go and tell more people about Jesus. God sent His angel to help Peter.

QUESTIONS:

1. *Does the angel have a key to the door?*
2. *What did the angel tell Peter to do?*

Acts 12:1-17

140

675

O H, WHAT IS HAPPENING to this man? He is kneeling down and praying while the bad men are killing him with big stones. Is he crying? No. He is praying and asking God not to hurt these men even though they are hurting him. These men are angry because Stephen told them about Jesus. They don't want to hear about Jesus and so they decided to kill Stephen. Stephen is happy because he sees Jesus up there in Heaven. In a little while he will go there and be with Jesus.

QUESTIONS:

1. *What is the man's name?*
2. *Why are these men throwing big stones at him?*

Acts 6:8-15; 7:54-60

THE MAN SITTING in the chariot and reading the Book wants to know more about God. He is reading part of the Bible. He has stopped the horses and is talking to Philip. Philip is one of Jesus' disciples. The Holy Spirit told him to run over to the chariot and start talking to the man. He is telling the man what the Bible means. He is telling him about Jesus. Soon the man sitting in the chariot will be a Christian.

QUESTIONS:

1. *What is the man's name who is standing there?*
2. *Who is he talking about?*
3. *Will the other man become a Christian?*

Acts 8:26-40

144

THIS MAN'S NAME IS PAUL. He doesn't like Christians. He would like to kill all of them or put them in jail. He is walking down the road trying to find some Christians to hurt. He thinks that all Christians are bad. He does not know that Jesus is God's Son. Paul thinks God likes him to hurt Christians. But soon God will tell Paul to love Jesus and His people. Then Paul won't hurt them any more.

QUESTIONS:

1. *What is this man's name?*
2. *Why does he hurt the Christians?*

Acts 9:1, 2

146

645

**ERE IS ANOTHER PICTURE** of Paul. While he was walking down the road all of a sudden God started talking to him from Heaven. He is telling Paul not to hurt the Christians any more. He is saying, "Paul, you too must become one of My friends. I am Jesus, and you must stop hurting Me and you must leave My people alone." Paul is very surprised and afraid, and is asking Jesus what He wants him to do. Jesus tells him and now Paul will always do whatever Jesus says.

QUESTIONS:

      1. Who is talking to Paul?
      2. Does Paul decide to love Jesus?

Acts 9:3-19

641   C L WOODWARD

**W**HO IS THIS MAN in the basket? It is Paul. His friends are helping him to get away. Paul has been telling everyone about his new Friend Jesus and how much he loves Him. Paul doesn't hurt God's children any more. The people who don't like God try to catch Paul so his friends are helping him to run away. Paul is God's friend now and he loves Jesus.

QUESTIONS:

1. *Who is the man in the basket?*
2. *Why is he running away?*

Acts 9:22-28

AUL AND SILAS are in jail but they don't care very much because they know that God loves them. They don't care what happens to them so they have been singing. All of a sudden a great earthquake shakes the jail and all of the doors swing open and the chains fall off their hands and feet so that they can run away. But they are not trying to run away. They are staying there and talking to the man who is supposed to keep them in jail. He is kneeling there asking them what to do. They are telling him to believe on Jesus and he will be saved.

QUESTIONS:

1. *Where are Paul and Silas?*
2. *Who are they talking to?*
3. *What did they tell the man to do?*

Acts 16:22-34

P AUL IS ON A BOAT and there is a great storm. Do you see the waves and how the ship is sinking? But God took care of Paul and all the people who were with him and none of them were hurt. They came through the water and got to the shore all right. Paul is standing there telling God, "Thank You," for taking care of them. God loves Paul, and God loves you.

QUESTIONS:

1. *Did the ship sink?*
2. *Were the people saved?*
3. *Does God love you?*

Acts 27:14-44

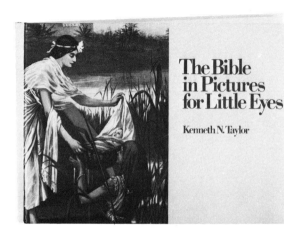

A larger volume by Kenneth N. Taylor, *The Bible in Pictures for Little Eyes,* includes stories from the Old Testament as well as the New. This classic has been in print for more than thirty years. Today it is published in fifty-four languages and has sold more than 1.5 million copies.